COOKING WITH
CHOCOLATE

BY NANCY LAMBERT

TOP THAT

Licensed exclusively to Top That Publishing Ltd
Tide Mill Way, Woodbridge, Suffolk, IP12 1AP, UK
www.topthatpublishing.com
Copyright © 2013 Tide Mill Media
All rights reserved
0 2 4 6 8 9 7 5 3 1
Printed and bound in China

CONTENTS

Introduction 5

Equipment, Safety and Hygiene 7

Getting Started 9

Chocolate & Orange Cookies 10

Chocolate & Ginger Cheesecake 11

Viennese Hot Chocolate 12

Chocolate Truffles 13

Chocolate Roulade 14

Mini Chocolate Meringues 15

Berry & White Chocolate Muffins 16

White Chocolate & Exotic Fruit Cookies 17

Chocolate Fondue 18

Chocolate Milkshake 19

Courgette & Chocolate Loaf 20

Sicilian Cassata 21

Chocolate Soufflé 22

White Chocolate Cake 23

Chocolate Florentines 24

Nutty Chocolate Fudge 25

Chocolate Ice Cream 26

Chocolate-Chip Cupcakes 27

Chocolate Tartlets 28

White Chocolate Pistachio Mousse 29

Chocolate & Peanut Butter Cookies 30

Chocolate Pancakes 31

Hot Chocolate Ice Cream Cake 32

Fruity Chocolate Crumble 33

Chocolate Coated Nuts 34

Mini Chocolate Cupcakes 35

Baci di Dama **36**

Classic Hot Chocolate **37**

Chocolate & Raspberry Cake **38**

Chocolate Ice Cream Sundae **39**

Chocolate Pots **40**

Chocolate Fudge Brownies **41**

Raspberry Chocolate Cupcakes **42**

Chocolate Macarons **43**

Chocolate Trifle **44**

Chocolate Meringue Nests **45**

Chocolate Almond Bars **46**

Chocolate-Chip Cookies **47**

Xocolatl **48**

Chocolate-Chip Cheesecake **49**

Chocolate & Peanut Butter Cupcakes **50**

Chocolate Mousse **51**

Chocolate & Almond Fridge Cake **52**

Choc Pops **53**

Chocolate Party Biscuits **54**

Chocolate Celebration Cake **55**

Chocolate Apples **56**

Marble Cake **57**

Mint Chocolate Cupcakes **58**

Hot Choca Mocha **59**

Chocolate Eggs **60**

Chocolate Pinwheel Cookies **61**

Chocolate Rice Pudding **62**

Chocolate Profiteroles **63**

Index of Recipes **64**

INTRODUCTION

Today, it is impossible to imagine a world without chocolate! Its history can be traced back to the ancient peoples of Central and South America and for thousands of years, chocolate has been credited with mystical powers.

The first chocolate bar, as we know them today, was created by English chocolate manufacturer, Joseph Fry & Son. In 1847, managed by the founder's great-grandson, Fry & Son developed a way of mixing cacao butter, sugar and cocoa powder to create a paste that could be formed into a solid chocolate bar, thereby creating the world's first eating chocolate.

This book will provide you with a selection of delicious chocolate recipes, for adults and junior chefs to make together. And remember, once you have perfected the recipes, don't be afraid to experiment with the ingredients, fillings and toppings to create your own chocolatey treats!

COOKING TIPS!

- Make sure you use the freshest ingredients possible.

- Always use the best quality chocolate you can. When buying chocolate, look at the percentage of cocoa solids, as this indicates the quality and taste of the chocolate – the higher, the better.

- Store chocolate in a cool, dry place.

- Chopping chocolate helps it melt more quickly and evenly.

EQUIPMENT

- To complete the recipes in this book, you will need to use a selection of everyday cooking equipment and utensils, such as mixing bowls, saucepans, a sieve, knives, spoons, forks and a chopping board.

- Of course, you'll need to weigh and measure the ingredients, so you'll need a measuring jug and some kitchen scales too.

- Some of the recipes tell you to use a whisk. Ask an adult to help you use an electric whisk, or you can use a balloon whisk yourself – you'll just have to work extra hard!

- To make some of the recipes in this book, you'll need to use the correct-sized tins or other special equipment. These items (and others that you may not have to hand) are listed at the start of each recipe.

SAFETY & HYGIENE

- Before starting any cooking always wash your hands.

- Cover any cuts with a plaster.

- Wear an apron to protect your clothes.

- Always make sure that all the equipment you use is clean.

- If you need to use a sharp knife to cut up something hard, ask an adult to help you. Always use a chopping board.

!
ADULT SUPERVISION
IS REQUIRED FOR
ALL RECIPES

- Remember that trays in the oven and pans on the cooker can get very hot. Always ask an adult to turn on the oven and to get things in and out of the oven for you.

- Always ask an adult for help if you are using anything electrical – like an electric whisk.

- Be careful when heating anything in a pan on top of the cooker. Keep the handle turned to one side to avoid accidentally knocking the pan.

- Keep your pets out of the kitchen while cooking.

GETTING STARTED

MEASURING

Use scales to weigh exactly how much of each ingredient you need or use a measuring jug to measure liquids.

MIXING

Use a spoon, balloon whisk or electric hand whisk to mix the ingredients together.

DIFFERENT IDEAS

Decorate your chocolate treats with flavoured or coloured icing, and then add chocolate drops, sweets or sugar strands.

CREATING RECIPES

Once you've made a chocolate recipe in this book a few times, think about whether you could make your own version. Try to think up names for the things you create!

PLEASE NOTE

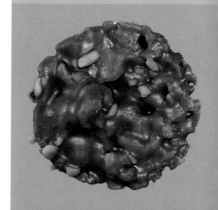

The measurements given in this book are approximate. Use the same measurement conversions throughout your recipe (grams or ounces) to maintain the correct ratios. All of the recipes in this book have been created for adults to make with junior chefs and must not be attempted by an unsupervised child.

Read through each recipe to make sure you've got all the ingredients that you need before you start.

CHOCOLATE & ORANGE COOKIES

Extra equipment:

- 2 baking trays
- baking parchment
- rolling pin
- cookie cutter

Ingredients:

- 150 g (5 oz) butter, softened
- 50 g (2 oz) brown sugar
- 225 g (8 oz) plain flour
- 50 g (2 oz) cocoa powder
- 2 teaspoons baking powder
- 75 g (3 oz) dark chocolate, chopped
- grated zest of 2 oranges
- 2 tablespoons orange juice

1 Preheat the oven to 180°C / 350°F / gas mark 4.

2 Line two baking trays with baking parchment.

3 Beat the butter and brown sugar together until the mixture is pale and fluffy.

4 In a separate bowl, sift the flour, cocoa powder and baking powder together and then carefully fold them into the butter and sugar mixture.

5 Add the chopped dark chocolate, orange zest and orange juice to the mixture and gently mix to form a smooth dough.

6 On a lightly-floured surface, roll out the dough to a thickness of 0.5 cm (1/4 in.). Cut it into approximately 30 biscuits with a cookie cutter.

7 Cook in the centre of the oven for 12–15 minutes.

8 Allow the biscuits to cool for five minutes before transferring them to a wire rack.

TOP TIP!
To keep your cookies fresh, store them in an airtight container when cold.

10

CHOCOLATE & GINGER CHEESECAKE

Extra equipment:
- 20 cm (8 in) springform tin
- baking parchment
- clean plastic bag
- rolling pin

Ingredients:
- 200 g (7 oz) ginger biscuits
- 75 g (3 oz) butter
- 25 g (1 oz) cocoa powder
- 600 g (1 lb 5 oz) mascarpone
- 1 tablespoon cold milk
- 50 g (2 oz) icing sugar, sifted
- 1/2 tablespoon stem ginger syrup
- 75 g (3 oz) dark chocolate, finely grated
- crystallised stem ginger, to decorate (optional)

1 Grease a 20 cm (8 in) loose-bottomed springform tin with butter and line the base with baking parchment.

2 Place the ginger biscuits in a strong plastic bag and crush them into fine crumbs with a rolling pin.

3 Ask an adult to melt the butter in a microwave, then add the biscuit crumbs and cocoa powder. Stir well.

4 Press the biscuit mixture firmly into the base of the tin.

5 Beat together the mascarpone, milk, sifted icing sugar and half a tablespoon of ginger syrup. Then, stir in the finely grated dark chocolate.

6 Spoon the mixture onto the biscuit base and refrigerate for at least one hour.

7 To serve, remove the cheesecake from the tin and decorate it with a few thinly sliced pieces of crystallised ginger (optional).

TOP TIP! Decorate with sweets if you don't like crystallised ginger.

VIENNESE HOT CHOCOLATE

Extra equipment:
- whisk

Ingredients:
- 150 g (5 oz) dark chocolate, broken into pieces
- 500 ml (17 fl.oz) whole milk
- 1 egg yolk
- 50 ml (2 fl.oz) whipped cream
- grated chocolate, to serve

1. Ask an adult to melt the dark chocolate in a small amount of water in a saucepan.

2. Add the milk and gently heat for a few minutes.

3. Take the mixture off the heat and allow it to cool.

4. Beat the egg yolk in a separate bowl, and then add to the saucepan.

5. Reheat the mixture for two minutes, being careful not to let it boil, stirring continuously.

6. Off the heat, whisk the mixture into a froth and serve.

7. Finish with a generous helping of whipped cream and some finely grated chocolate.

TOP TIP!
This drink will be very hot! Let it cool for a few minutes before drinking!

CHOCOLATE TRUFFLES

Extra equipment:
- sweet cases
- plastic container

Ingredients:
- 150 g (6 oz) plain chocolate
- 150 ml (5 fl.oz) double cream
- 25 g (1 oz) butter

To coat the truffles any of the following:
- cocoa powder
- chocolate strands
- chopped nuts

1 Ask an adult to put a heatproof bowl over a saucepan of just-simmering water, making sure the bowl doesn't touch the water. Break the plain chocolate into small pieces and put it into the bowl, and then add the cream and butter. Stir the mixture until the chocolate has melted.

2 Take the saucepan off the heat. Take the bowl off the saucepan and leave it to cool for a few minutes. Carefully pour the melted chocolate into a plastic container. Put the lid on the container and leave it in the fridge to set for 3–4 hours.

3 Remove the container from the fridge. Roll small balls of the chocolate truffle mixture in your hands.

4 Roll the balls in cocoa powder, chocolate strands or chopped nuts, and then put them into the sweet cases.

5 Store the truffles in a container in the fridge until you're ready to eat them or give them as a gift.

TOP TIP!
You'll have to roll the truffle balls quickly or the mixture will melt in your hands!

CHOCOLATE ROULADE

SERVES 8

Extra equipment:
- 33 x 23 cm (13 x 9 in) swiss roll tin
- baking parchment
- greaseproof paper

Ingredients:
- 200 g (7 oz) plain chocolate, broken into pieces
- 150 g (5 oz) caster sugar
- 5 eggs, separated

For the filling:
- 100 g (4 oz) white chocolate, broken into pieces
- 284 ml (9 1/2 fl.oz) double cream
- 2 tablespoons icing sugar, to decorate

1 Preheat the oven to 180°C / 350°F / gas mark 4.

2 Put the tin on a sheet of baking parchment and cut around it, leaving an edge of 2.5 cm (1 in). Grease the tin with some butter, then fit the paper into the tin, folding in the edges. Finally, grease the paper with butter.

3 Ask an adult to put a heatproof bowl over a saucepan of just-simmering water, making sure the bowl doesn't touch the water. Put the plain chocolate in the bowl and melt until smooth.

4 Whisk the sugar and the egg yolks in a separate bowl until very thick, then fold in the chocolate.

5 In a separate bowl, whisk the egg whites until stiff. Beat 2 tablespoons of the egg whites into the chocolate mixture, and then fold in the remainder.

6 Pour the mixture into the tin and bake for 15–20 minutes until risen. Leave to cool. Sift the icing sugar onto a sheet of greaseproof paper, then turn out the roulade onto it.

7 Melt the white chocolate, repeating the same process as earlier. Cool for 5 minutes, then whip the cream, before folding it into the melted chocolate. Remove the baking parchment from the roulade, then spread over the cream mixture. Now roll it up!

MINI CHOCOLATE MERINGUES

Extra equipment:
- 2 baking trays
- greaseproof paper
- whisk
- sieve
- piping bag

Ingredients:
- 3 egg whites
- 150 g (5 oz) caster sugar
- 50 g (2 oz) dark chocolate, grated
- 2 teaspoons cocoa powder

1 Preheat the oven to 140°C / 275°F / gas mark 1.

2 Line two baking trays with greaseproof paper.

3 Next, whisk three egg whites until soft peaks form, then gradually whisk in the caster sugar until stiff peaks form.

4 Stir together the dark chocolate and sifted cocoa powder and fold gently into the meringue mixture.

5 Place the mixture into a piping bag and squeeze 3.5 cm (1 1/2 in) 'blobs' of the mixture onto the baking trays and ask an adult to quickly place them into the oven for 40 minutes.

6 Once cool, dust with cocoa powder, and serve.

TOP TIP!
To separate the egg white from the yolk, crack the egg lightly, then hold half the shell, with the yolk in it, in one hand, and the other half-shell in the other. Allow as much of the egg white as possible to run out of the shell and down into a bowl, then transfer the yolk to the other half of the shell, allowing more of the white to run out.

BERRY & WHITE CHOCOLATE MUFFINS

Extra equipment:

- muffin tray
- muffin cases

Ingredients:

- 200 g (7 oz) self-raising flour
- 100 g (4 oz) caster sugar
- 2 teaspoons dried coffee granules
- 2 eggs
- 1 tablespoon extra virgin olive oil
- 150 ml (5 fl.oz) whole milk
- 100 g (4 oz) white chocolate, broken into small chunks
- 100 g (4 oz) fresh or frozen mixed forest berries
- 1 grated dessert apple

1 Preheat the oven to 200°C / 400°F / gas mark 6. Place the muffin cases in the muffin tray.

2 Sift the flour into a large mixing bowl, then mix in the sugar and coffee granules. Make a 'well' in the middle.

3 In a separate bowl, beat together the eggs, oil and milk.

4 Add the egg mixture to the well in the flour bowl and mix it roughly, ignoring any lumps. Then, add the white chocolate chunks, berries and grated apple.

5 Mix all of the ingredients together roughly. Do not over-mix.

6 Spoon immediately into the muffin cases, so that they are two thirds full.

7 Ask an adult to place the tray in the centre of the oven for 20–25 minutes. Allow the muffins to cool for 5 minutes before removing them from the tin.

TOP TIP!
Muffins are best enjoyed warm. Any leftover muffins can be reheated for a few minutes in the oven the next day.

WHITE CHOCOLATE & EXOTIC FRUIT COOKIES

Extra equipment:

- 2 baking trays
- baking parchment

Ingredients:

- 200 g (7 oz) plain flour
- 1 teaspoon baking powder
- 100 g (4 oz) unsalted butter
- 100 g (4 oz) light brown sugar
- 80 g (3 oz) white chocolate, chopped
- 80 g (3 oz) of mixed exotic dried fruit (papaya, pineapple, mango etc) chopped
- 1 teaspoon lemon zest
- 1 egg

1 Preheat the oven to 190°C / 375°F / gas mark 5. Line two baking trays with lightly greased baking parchment.

2 Sift the flour and baking powder into a bowl. Rub the butter into the flour with your fingertips.

3 Mix in the sugar, chopped chocolate and dried fruit.

4 Add the lemon zest and egg, plus a little extra water if necessary, and mix to form a soft dough.

5 Place spoonfuls of the mixture on the baking trays, leaving a space between each one.

6 Ask an adult to place the trays in the oven for 10–12 minutes until the cookies are a light, golden brown.

7 Allow to cool for 5 minutes, then transfer to a wire rack. Store in an airtight container.

TOP TIP!
Double the ingredients to make double the cookies!

CHOCOLATE FONDUE

Extra equipment:
- fondue pot and fork

Ingredients:
- 340 g (12 oz) good-quality plain chocolate
- 300 ml (10 fl.oz) double cream

To serve
- fresh fruit — strawberries, pineapple chunks, peach slices, grapes, etc.
- This fondue recipe tastes great when served with other recipes from this book. Why not try dipping the chocolate orange cookies (p. 10), chocolate & peanut butter cookies (p. 30) or mini chocolate meringues (p. 15) for a chocoholic overdose!

1 Break up the chocolate into the fondue pot.

2 Add the double cream and ask an adult to heat gently, stirring all the time until the chocolate has melted.

3 Serve with fruit, cookies and other sweet treats for dipping.

TOP TIP!
Why not add a little grated orange peel to make chocolate orange fondue!

CHOCOLATE MILKSHAKE

Extra equipment:
• blender

Ingredients:
• 2 tablespoons dark chocolate powder
• 200 ml (7 fl.oz) chilled milk
• 2 rounded tablespoons vanilla ice cream

1 First, place the dark chocolate powder into a jug followed by a small amount of milk. Place in a microwave and heat for about 20 seconds, or until the powder has dissolved into the milk. Stir well.

2 Next, add the rest of the milk, then the ice cream. Give the mixture a good stir, or place in a blender and ask an adult to process until smooth. Place in the fridge.

3 Once cool, pour into a glass and serve!

TOP TIP!
Add more milk if you'd like a thinner shake!

19

COURGETTE & CHOCOLATE LOAF

Extra equipment:

• 1 kg (2 lb) loaf tin

Ingredients:

• 175 g (6 oz) butter, softened
• 150 g (5 oz) soft brown sugar
• 3 eggs, beaten
• 1 medium courgette, grated
• 50 g (2 oz) chocolate chips
• 50 g (2 oz) marzipan,
  finely chopped
• 175 g (6 oz) self-raising flour
• 50 g (2 oz) cocoa powder

1 Preheat the oven to 180°C / 350°F / gas mark 4.

2 Grease the loaf tin with a little butter.

3 Cream the butter and sugar together until the mixture is fluffy and pale, then add the beaten eggs, one at a time. Mix well.

4 Now add the grated courgette, chocolate chips and chopped marzipan, and mix.

5 Sift together the flour and cocoa powder, and fold into the mixture.

6 Transfer the mixture to the loaf tin and bake for 50–55 minutes or until firm to touch.

7 Allow the loaf to cool for 15 minutes, then serve warm.

TOP TIP!
Set a timer so you don't forget about your loaf in the oven!

20

SICILIAN CASSATA

Extra equipment:
- large pudding basin
- plate or heavy weight

Ingredients:
- 1 Victoria sponge
- 450 g (1 lb) ricotta
- 30 ml (1 fl.oz) milk
- 225 g (8 oz) caster sugar
- 225 g (8 oz) Italian candied fruit, finely chopped
- 100 g (4 oz) dark chocolate, roughly grated

To decorate:
- 100 g (4 oz) dark chocolate, broken into pieces
- 25 g (1 oz) butter
- 50 g (2 oz) candied fruit (optional)

1 Ask an adult to cut the sponge into thin, flat slices. Use the slices to line a large pudding basin, keeping a few to one side.

2 Beat the ricotta with the milk until smooth. Then mix in the sugar, candied fruit and roughly grated dark chocolate.

3 Pour the ricotta mixture into the basin and finish with a layer of sponge.

4 Place a plate or heavy weight on top of the basin and refrigerate the cassata for four to five hours.

5 For the decoration, ask an adult to put a heatproof bowl over a saucepan of just-simmering water. Make sure the bowl doesn't touch the water.

6 Add the chocolate and butter and stir until it has melted. Then, allow the mixture to cool until it begins to thicken.

7 Turn the cassata out onto a decorative plate and drizzle over the melted chocolate. Put it back in the fridge for at least one hour.

8 Top with pieces of candied fruit if desired. Serve very cold.

TOP TIP!
Don't be afraid to add lots of chocolate topping to your cassata!

CHOCOLATE SOUFFLÉ

TOP TIP! Make sure the oven is the correct temperature before placing the soufflés inside!

Extra equipment:

- 8 soufflé dishes
- sieve
- whisk

Ingredients:

- butter, for greasing
- sugar, for dusting
- 500 ml (17 fl.oz) milk
- 125 g (4 ½ oz) caster sugar
- 225 g (8 oz) chopped plain chocolate
- 6 large egg whites
- 4 large egg yolks
- icing sugar, to decorate

1 Preheat the oven to 180°C / 350°F / gas mark 4.

2 Grease eight soufflé dishes with a little butter. Sprinkle with sugar and then tap out the excess.

3 Ask an adult to bring the milk and 100 g (4 oz) of caster sugar to a simmer in a saucepan, stirring occasionally until the sugar has dissolved. Reduce the heat to low.

4 Add the chopped plain chocolate and stir until smooth.

5 Pour into a large bowl and allow to cool for 10 minutes.

6 Beat the egg whites in a separate bowl until they form soft peaks. Slowly add the remaining sugar and beat until stiff but not dry.

7 Whisk the egg yolks into the chocolate mixture. Whisk a quarter of the egg whites into the chocolate mixture to lighten. Then, fold in the remaining egg whites.

8 Divide the mixture among the prepared soufflé dishes. Bake them in a preheated oven for about 15 minutes, until the soufflés puff up.

9 Sift icing sugar over the tops and serve warm.

WHITE CHOCOLATE CAKE

Extra equipment:
- 2 x 20 cm (8 in) loose-bottomed sandwich tins
- baking parchment
- spatula

Ingredients:
- 200 g (7 oz) butter, softened
- 200 g (7 oz) golden caster sugar
- 200 g (7 oz) self-raising flour
- 50 g (2 oz) ground almonds
- 2 eggs, beaten
- 2 egg yolks, beaten
- 2 tablespoons milk

For the filling:
- 600 g (1 lb 5 oz) mascarpone
- 50 ml (2 fl.oz) milk
- 175 g (6 oz) icing sugar, sifted
- grated zest and juice of 2 limes
- 75 g (3 oz) white chocolate, grated

1 Preheat the oven to 160°C / 325°F / gas mark 3. Line the base of the sandwich tins with baking parchment.

2 Put all of the sponge ingredients in a bowl, then beat until creamy and well mixed.

3 Divide the mixture between the two sandwich tins and level the tops with a spoon or spatula.

4 Bake both cakes for about 40 minutes or until golden brown. (Use a knife to check that your sponge is cooked in the middle. If the knife comes out clean, then your cake is ready.) Ask an adult to remove the cakes from the tins and cool on a wire rack.

5 Place all of the ingredients for the cream filling into a bowl and mix well. Refrigerate for 30 minutes before using.

6 Spread the filling onto the top of one of the sponges with a spatula and place the other sponge on top. Continue spreading the filling over the top and sides of the cake to finish.

TOP TIP!
Invest in a cake stand so you can show off your chocolatey creations!

CHOCOLATE FLORENTINES

TOP TIP!
Why not add some candied fruit for a fruity alternative to nuts?

Extra equipment:
- 2 baking trays
- greaseproof paper

Ingredients:
- 60 ml (2 fl.oz) milk
- 75 g (3 oz) butter
- 100 g (4 oz) icing sugar
- 50 g (2 oz) plain flour
- 50 g (2 oz) chopped nuts
- 50 g (2 oz) flaked almonds

For the chocolate coating:
- 100 g (4 oz) dark, milk or white chocolate
- 10 g (¹/₃ oz) unsalted butter

1 Preheat the oven to 190°C / 375°F / gas mark 4. Line two baking trays with greaseproof paper.

2 In a saucepan, ask an adult to heat the milk, butter and icing sugar, stirring until the sugar has dissolved.

3 Off the heat, add the plain flour, chopped nuts and flaked almonds. Allow the mixture to go cold.

4 Spoon small quantities of the mixture onto the baking trays. Allow plenty of space between them as the mixture spreads when it is cooking.

5 Cook for about 7–10 minutes until golden brown.

6 Leave to cool for ten minutes, then carefully transfer to a wire cooling rack.

7 Ask an adult to put a heatproof bowl over a saucepan of just-simmering water. Make sure the bowl doesn't touch the water. Add the chocolate and butter and stir until they have melted. Melt a different type of chocolate in a separate bowl if you wish.

8 Dip each florentine into the chocolate so the base and sides are covered in the chocolate mixture. Allow them to cool completely, chocolate side up.

NUTTY CHOCOLATE FUDGE

Extra equipment:
- 15 cm (6 in) square baking tin
- greaseproof paper

Ingredients:
- 300 g (10 oz) plain chocolate
- 200 ml (7 fl.oz) condensed milk
- 2 teaspoons vanilla essence
- 100 g (4 oz) walnuts, chopped

1 Line the tin with greaseproof paper.

2 Ask an adult to help you put the plain chocolate, condensed milk and vanilla essence into a saucepan over a medium heat. Stir them together until the chocolate has melted.

3 Add the chopped walnuts and stir until evenly combined.

4 Ask an adult to pour the mixture into the tin, and smooth the top with the back of a spoon. Put the tin into the fridge for 3–4 hours.

5 Remove the fudge from the tin by lifting it with the greaseproof paper. Turn it out onto a board and peel off the paper.

6 Cut the slab of fudge into squares and serve!

TOP TIP!
Add white or dark chocolate to make different flavoured fudge!

CHOCOLATE ICE CREAM

TOP TIP!
Add some chocolate chips to the mixture for an extra treat!

MAKES APPROX 1 LITRE

Extra equipment:
- electric whisk
- ice cream maker (optional)

Ingredients:
- 300 g (10 oz) dark chocolate, finely chopped
- 240 ml (8 fl.oz) milk
- 240 ml (8 fl.oz) double cream
- 175 g (6 oz) caster sugar
- 4 large egg yolks
- 150 ml (5 fl.oz) water

1 First, tip 200 g (7 oz) of dark chocolate into a heatproof bowl, reserving the rest to add to the ice cream later. Heat the milk, double cream and 25 g (1 oz) of caster sugar in a saucepan, then pour over the chocolate and stir until dissolved. Leave on one side until cool.

2 Ask an adult to whisk the egg yolks with an electric whisk and add this to the cooled chocolate cream mixture.

3 Next, place 150 g (5 oz) of sugar in a saucepan and add 150 ml (5 fl.oz) of water. Dissolve the sugar over a medium heat, stirring occasionally. Then, bring to a boil and cook for 5 minutes.

4 Ask an adult to pour the hot sugar syrup into the chocolate cream mixture, in a thin steady stream, whilst you whisk. Continue whisking until the mixture has thickened and is similar to a mousse – this should take about 5 minutes.

5 Add the extra chocolate and stir to blend everything together. Pour into an ice cream maker and churn until frozen. Alternatively, you could freeze the mixture in a tub, stirring it every hour to break up any ice and ensure that the chocolate is evenly mixed in.

6 Once it is frozen, scoop and serve!

CHOCOLATE-CHIP CUPCAKES

Extra equipment:
- bun tin
- sieve
- bun cases

Ingredients:
- 100 g (4 oz) self-raising flour
- 1 tablespoon cocoa powder
- 125 g (4 ½ oz) butter, softened
- 125 g (4 ½ oz) caster sugar
- 2 large eggs
- 2–3 tablespoons milk
- 50 g (2 oz) chocolate chips

1 Preheat the oven to 180°C / 350°F / gas mark 4.

2 Sift the self-raising flour and cocoa powder into a bowl.

3 Put the butter in the bowl. Use the tips of your fingers to rub the butter, flour and cocoa powder together until the mixture becomes crumbly.

4 Add the caster sugar and mix it in, then stir in the large eggs.

5 Finally, add the milk to make the mixture creamy, followed by the chocolate chips. Stir to mix.

6 Put spoonfuls of the mixture into the bun cases. Bake the cupcakes for 10–15 minutes, then leave them to cool on a wire rack.

7 Once cool, top the cupcakes with more chocolate chips or leave plain.

TOP TIP! Why not try white chocolate chips for a yummy alternative!

CHOCOLATE TARTLETS

Ingredients:
- 6 pre-cooked and ready-made pastry tartlet cases

For the filling:
- 200 g (7 oz) dark chocolate
- 284 ml (9 1/2 fl.oz) carton double cream
- 100 ml (3 fl.oz) milk
- 2 large eggs
- 100 g (4 oz) caster sugar
- a few drops of vanilla essence

For the topping:
- cocoa powder
- whipped cream
- caramelised fruit

1 Place the pre-cooked, ready-made pastry tartlet cases onto serving plates.

2 To make the filling, ask an adult to put a heatproof bowl over a saucepan of just-simmering water, making sure the bowl doesn't touch the water. Break the chocolate into small pieces and put them in the bowl. Stir until melted.

3 Ask an adult to bring the cream and milk to the boil in a pan, then pour in the melted chocolate, stirring until smooth.

4 Whisk together the eggs, sugar and vanilla, then mix with the chocolate cream. Leave to cool.

5 Once cool, spoon the chocolate filling into the pastry cases.

6 Dust the tartlets with cocoa powder. Top with a dollop of whipped cream and a piece of caramelised fruit.

TOP TIP!
When you become more confident at cooking, try making your own pastry tartlet cases.

28

WHITE CHOCOLATE PISTACHIO MOUSSE

Extra equipment:
• electric whisk
• 4 dessert glasses

Ingredients:
• 3 tablespoons water
• a few drops of vanilla essence
• 180 g (6 oz) white chocolate, grated
• 2 separated, fresh eggs (pasteurised if possible)
• 300 ml (10 fl.oz) whipping cream
• 45 g (1 ½ oz) pistachio nuts, chopped
• whole pistachio nuts, to decorate
• 45 g (1 ½ oz) white chocolate, grated, to decorate

1 Place the water, vanilla essence and white chocolate in a bowl over a second bowl filled with hot water until the chocolate has melted. Stir until smooth, then whisk in the egg yolks.

2 In a clean bowl, whisk the egg whites until they make soft peaks.

3 Lightly beat the cream and fold two thirds into the chocolate mixture, followed by the egg whites.

4 Place a spoonful in the bottom of four glasses. Sprinkle with chopped pistachios, then add another layer of mousse. Alternate mousse and pistachio layers until the glasses are full.

5 Finish whipping the remaining cream and place a spoonful on the top of each glass.

6 Decorate with whole pistachios and grated white chocolate to finish.

TOP TIP! Keep the mousses in the fridge until they are ready to be eaten!

CHOCOLATE & PEANUT BUTTER COOKIES

Extra equipment:

- baking tray
- greaseproof paper
- sieve

Ingredients:

- 125 g (4 ¹/₂ oz) butter, softened
- 50 g (2 oz) smooth peanut butter
- 75 g (3 oz) sugar
- 2 large free-range eggs, beaten
- 1 teaspoon vanilla essence
- 200 g (7 oz) plain flour
- 1 teaspoon baking powder
- 75 g (3 oz) dark chocolate, chopped
- 50 g (2 oz) unsalted peanuts
- 1–2 tablespoons milk (optional)

1 Preheat the oven to 180°C / 350°F / gas mark 4.

2 Grease and line a baking tray with greaseproof paper.

3 Beat together the butter, smooth peanut butter and sugar until the mixture is light and fluffy.

4 Add the beaten eggs and vanilla essence, and mix well.

5 Sift the plain flour and baking powder together and fold them into the mixture.

6 Add the chunks of chopped dark chocolate and the peanuts.

7 Mix in 1–2 tablespoonfuls of milk if the dough appears too stiff.

8 Place evenly spaced spoonfuls of the mixture onto the baking tray, pressing each one down with the back of a spoon. (Dipping the spoon into water will stop it sticking to the dough.)

9 Place the cookies in the centre of a preheated oven for 20 minutes, or until golden brown. Allow them to cool before serving.

TOP TIP! To soften the butter, take it out of the fridge at least 30 minutes before cooking.

CHOCOLATE PANCAKES

Extra equipment:
- whisk

Ingredients:
- 85 g (3 oz) self-raising flour
- 1 egg
- 300 ml (10 fl.oz) milk (approx)
- oil, for frying

For the chocolate sauce:
- 50 g (2 oz) caster sugar
- splash hot water
- 25 g (1 oz) cocoa powder

1 To make the pancakes, whisk the flour, egg and milk in a bowl to make a smooth batter.

2 Ask an adult to heat the oil in a frying pan and ladle half of the mixture in. Allow the mixture to coat the pan and fry the pancake for 1–2 minutes on each side or until golden.

3 Repeat to make another pancake.

4 For the sauce, ask an adult to whisk the sugar, water and cocoa together in a small pan over a gentle heat. Add extra water depending on how thick you require the sauce.

5 To serve, transfer the pancakes to a plate and drizzle the chocolate sauce over.

TOP TIP! Place a handful of berries on top of the pancakes, then drizzle with chocolate sauce!

HOT CHOCOLATE ICE CREAM CAKE

Extra equipment:
- baking tray
- baking parchment

Ingredients:
- 4 egg whites
- 100 g (4 oz) icing sugar
- 1 Victoria sponge
- chocolate ice cream
- vanilla ice cream

① Preheat the oven to 200°C / 400°F / gas mark 6.

② Line a baking tray with baking parchment.

③ In a clean bowl, beat the egg whites with half the icing sugar until stiff peaks are formed.

④ Fold in the remaining icing sugar, and beat the mixture until it is stiff and glossy to form a meringue mixture.

⑤ Working quickly, place a layer of chocolate ice cream on the sponge and a layer of vanilla ice cream on top.

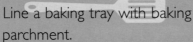

⑥ Next, cover the ice cream and cake with the meringue mixture.

⑦ Then, bake the dessert in the top of a hot oven for three to four minutes, then transfer it to a plate and serve immediately.

TOP TIP! Finish with a sprinkling of grated chocolate!

32

FRUITY CHOCOLATE CRUMBLE

Extra equipment:
- 1.5 litre (2 ½ pt) ovenproof dish
- 4 serving dishes

Ingredients:
- 3 pears, around 600 g (1 lb 3 oz)
- 3 Granny Smith apples, around 500 g (1 lb 1 oz)
- 100 g (4 oz) golden caster sugar
- 3 tablespoons water

For the crumble:
- 300 g (10 oz) plain flour
- 150 g (5 oz) brown sugar
- 200 g (7 oz) unsalted butter, cut into small cubes and chilled
- 100 g (4 oz) rolled oats
- 50 g (2 oz) dark chocolate, grated

1 Preheat the oven to 180°C / 350°F / gas mark 4, then lightly grease your ovenproof dish.

2 First, make the crumble. Put the flour, sugar and butter in a food processor and ask an adult to process until a fine powder. Put in a bowl and add the oats and chocolate. Mix together well, then chill.

3 Meanwhile, ask an adult to peel, core and slice the pears and apples. Lightly toss with golden caster sugar and pile into the ovenproof dish, levelling out the top. Spoon over the water.

4 Next, spread the crumble topping evenly and generously over the fruit.

5 Bake for 40–50 minutes until the fruit is bubbling hot and the topping is crispy.

6 Divide the crumble evenly between the dishes, and serve!

TOP TIP!
Use whatever fruit is available and takes your fancy. Why not try blackberries or rhubarb?

CHOCOLATE COATED NUTS

Extra equipment:
- 2 baking trays
- baking parchment

Ingredients:
- 150 g (5 oz) whole almonds
- 100 g (4 oz) milk chocolate

1 Preheat the oven to 220°C / 425°F / gas mark 7.

2 Place the almonds on a baking tray and roast in the oven for 5–10 minutes, or until they are lightly browned.

3 Next, place a piece of baking parchment on another baking tray.

4 Meanwhile, ask an adult to put a heatproof bowl over a saucepan of just-simmering water, making sure the bowl doesn't touch the water.

5 Break the chocolate into small pieces and put them in the bowl. Stir until melted.

6 Remove the chocolate from the heat and pour all of the almonds into the melted chocolate. Stir gently to coat the almonds in the chocolate.

7 Then, carefully remove the almonds, one by one, and place them on the baking tray.

8 Place the tray in the refrigerator for about 15 minutes for the chocolate to cool and harden.

TOP TIP!
Try melting white and dark chocolate for alternatives.

34

MINI CHOCOLATE CUPCAKES

Extra equipment:

- mini bun case baking tray
- mini paper bun cases
- sieve
- electric whisk (optional)

Ingredients:

- 125 g (4 ¹/₂ oz) self-raising flour
- 125 g (4 ¹/₂ oz) butter, softened
- 1 tablespoon cocoa powder
- 125 g (4 ¹/₂ oz) caster sugar
- 2 large eggs
- 2–3 tablespoons milk

For the topping:

- 150 g (5 oz) butter
- 150 g (5 oz) sifted icing sugar
- 4 tablespoons cocoa powder
- 3 tablespoons milk
- sugar sprinkles

1 Preheat the oven to 180°C / 350°F / gas mark 4.

2 Sift the flour into a bowl, followed by the butter. Use the tips of your fingers to rub the butter, flour and cocoa powder together until the mixture becomes crumbly. Alternatively, ask an adult to use an electric whisk.

3 Add the sugar and mix it in, then stir in the eggs. Finally, add the milk to make the mixture creamy.

4 Put spoonfuls of the mixture into the mini paper bun cases. Bake the cupcakes for 8–10 minutes, then leave them to cool on a wire rack.

5 For the topping, beat the butter in a large bowl until soft. Add half of the icing sugar and beat until smooth.

6 Add the remaining icing sugar, cocoa powder and one tablespoon of the milk and beat the mixture until creamy and smooth. Beat in more milk if necessary to loosen the icing.

7 Swirl the topping onto each of the cupcakes and finish with sugar sprinkles.

TOP TIP! Always allow your cupcakes to completely cool before decorating.

BACI DI DAMA

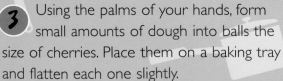

TOP TIP!
Allow the chocolate to cool completely before serving these delicious biscuits!

Extra equipment:
- 2 baking trays
- greaseproof paper

Ingredients:
- 150 g (5 oz) plain flour
- 150 g (5 oz) ground almonds
- 150 g (5 oz) caster sugar
- 125 g (4 ½ oz) butter
- 1 teaspoon vanilla essence
- 2–3 teaspoons water

For the filling:
- 200 g (7 oz) dark chocolate, chopped

1 Preheat the oven to 150°C / 300°F / gas mark 2. Line two baking trays with greaseproof paper.

2 In a large bowl, mix together the flour, ground almonds and sugar. Then, rub in the butter with your fingertips until it looks crumbly. Add the vanilla essence and sufficient water to just bind the ingredients, forming a stiff dough. Work the dough lightly for two to three minutes.

3 Using the palms of your hands, form small amounts of dough into balls the size of cherries. Place them on a baking tray and flatten each one slightly.

4 Cook them in the centre of the oven for 15–20 minutes until golden brown.

5 Allow them to cool on a wire rack.

6 Ask an adult to place a heatproof bowl over a bowl of gently simmering water and add the chopped chocolate. Heat until the chocolate has just melted, stirring gently. Be careful not to overheat.

7 Allow the chocolate to cool a little then, using a teaspoon, place a little of the melted chocolate onto one of the biscuits. Take another of the biscuits and press them together. Continue making biscuit 'sandwiches' until they have been used up.

CLASSIC HOT CHOCOLATE

SERVES 4

Ingredients:

- 1 litre (1 ¾ pt) full cream milk
- 1 vanilla pod
- 150 g (5 oz) milk chocolate, broken into pieces

1 Ask an adult to gently heat the milk with the vanilla pod.

2 Add the chocolate pieces.

3 Bring the mixture to the boil, stirring frequently.

4 Remove the vanilla pod and serve.

TOP TIP!
Top this drink with marshmallows – a campfire classic!

CHOCOLATE & RASPBERRY CAKE

TOP TIP!
Frozen raspberries can also be used – just defrost them before using!

Extra equipment:
- 23 cm (9 in) springform cake tin

Ingredients:
- 225 g (8 oz) butter
- 150 g (5 oz) sugar
- 3 free-range eggs, beaten
- 175 g (6 oz) self-raising flour
- 75 g (3 oz) cocoa powder
- 1 teaspoon vanilla essence
- 1 tablespoon milk

For the filling:
- 500 g (1 lb) mascarpone
- 15 ml (½ fl.oz) milk
- 225 g (8 oz) chocolate, broken into pieces
- 150 g (5 oz) sifted icing sugar
- 150 g (5 oz) raspberries

1 Preheat the oven to 180°C / 350°F / gas mark 4.

2 Grease a 23 cm (9 in) springform cake tin.

3 Cream together the butter and sugar and add the beaten eggs one at a time. Sift the flour and cocoa powder together and fold them into the mixture. Add the teaspoonful of vanilla essence and the milk.

4 Transfer the mixture to the cake tin and bake in the centre of the oven for 35–40 minutes. Allow the cake to cool on a wire cooling rack.

5 For the filling, beat the mascarpone and milk to form a smooth cream.

6 Ask an adult to put a heatproof bowl, containing the chocolate, over a saucepan of just-simmering water. Make sure the bowl doesn't touch the water. Stir until the chocolate has melted. Allow the chocolate to cool and then add it to the mascarpone. Add sifted icing sugar and mix well. Refrigerate for 30 minutes.

7 Cut the cake in half and spread one-third of the chocolate mascarpone on one side. Place half the raspberries on top of the chocolate and carefully replace the top half of the cake.

8 Use the rest of the mascarpone mixture to decorate the top and sides of the cake. Top the cake with the remaining raspberries.

CHOCOLATE ICE CREAM SUNDAE

Extra equipment:
- whisk
- grater
- 2 sundae glasses
- piping bag

Ingredients:
- 4 scoops chocolate ice cream (see home-made recipe on p.26 or use shop-bought)
- 50 g (2 oz) milk chocolate, grated
- 75 ml (3 fl.oz) whipped cream, to decorate
- glacé cherries, to decorate

For the hot chocolate sauce:
- 15 g ($^1/_2$ oz) cornflour
- 280 ml (10 fl.oz) milk
- 15 g ($^1/_2$ oz) butter
- 50 g (2 oz) sugar
- 50 g (2 oz) dark chocolate

1 First, make the hot chocolate sauce. Mix the cornflour with a little milk.

2 Boil the remaining milk, whisk in the cornflour mixture and add the butter and sugar.

3 Reboil carefully and grate the dark chocolate into the hot (but not boiling) sauce, and whisk until smooth.

4 Pour a small amount of the hot chocolate sauce into each sundae glass and top with a sprinkling of grated milk chocolate, then a scoop of chocolate ice cream. Repeat the process until the glass is full.

5 Place the whipped cream into a piping bag and pipe it onto the top of the sundae.

6 Finish with a glacé cherry.

TOP TIP!
Chopped nuts are a great addition to the cream topping.

CHOCOLATE POTS

Extra equipment:
- 6 ramekins
- whisk
- foil
- roasting tray

Ingredients:
- 2 eggs
- 2 egg yolks
- 15 g (1/2 oz) caster sugar
- 1 teaspoon cornflour
- 570 ml (1 pt) milk
- 100 g (4 oz) dark chocolate
- 4 tablespoons chocolate and hazelnut spread
- 100 ml (3 fl.oz) whipping cream, beaten until stiff
- grated chocolate, to decorate
- mint leaves, to decorate

1 Beat together the two eggs, egg yolks, sugar and cornflour until well mixed.

2 Ask an adult to heat the milk until nearly boiling. Gradually pour the hot milk onto the egg mixture whilst whisking.

3 Heat the dark chocolate and hazelnut spread in a bowl over warm water. When melted, whisk into the egg mixture.

4 Grease six small ramekins or ovenproof dishes and pour in equal portions of the mixture into each one. Cover the tops with foil and place in a roasting tray. Fill the tray with water halfway up the dishes, and place in a preheated oven at 160°C / 325°F / gas mark 3 for 30–40 minutes, or until the mixture sets.

5 Remove the ramekins from the tray and chill until required. Decorate the tops with whipped cream, a little grated dark chocolate and a mint leaf.

TOP TIP!
Make sure that the eggs used are very fresh and preferably free-range as this will improve the taste.

CHOCOLATE FUDGE BROWNIES

Extra equipment:

- sieve
- 20 cm (8 in) square cake tin
- baking parchment
- whisk

Ingredients:

- 2 eggs
- 225 g (8 oz) caster sugar
- 100 g (4 oz) butter
- 3 tablespoons cocoa powder
- 100 g (4 oz) self-raising flour
- 50 g (2 oz) pecans, chopped

For the topping:

- 50 g (2 oz) butter
- 1 tablespoon milk
- 100 g (4 oz) icing sugar
- 2 tablespoons cocoa powder
- pecan or walnut halves, to decorate

1 Preheat the oven to 180°C / 350°F / gas mark 4.

2 Beat the eggs and the sugar together in a bowl, until light and fluffy.

3 Melt the butter in the microwave (5 seconds max) and beat in the cocoa powder before adding to the eggs and sugar.

4 Sift the self-raising flour and fold into the main mixture with the chopped pecans.

5 Grease a 20 cm (8 in) square cake tin with butter, then line it with baking parchment. Pour in the mixture and bake in the oven for 40–45 minutes.

6 For the topping, melt the butter in a small pan and add the milk. Remove from the heat, then beat in the icing sugar and cocoa powder.

7 Spread icing over the cooked brownies and decorate with pecans or walnut halves. Cut into squares when the topping is firm.

TOP TIP!
If you don't like nuts, just remove them from the cooking process!

RASPBERRY CHOCOLATE CUPCAKES

TOP TIP!
Serve with an ice cold drink on a hot day or a warming hot chocolate on a chilly day!

MAKES 10–12

Extra equipment:
- bun tin and bun cases
- piping bag

Ingredients:
- 50 g (2 oz) dark chocolate
- 120 ml (4 fl.oz) water
- 2 eggs
- 225 g (8 oz) brown sugar
- 100 g (4 oz) butter, softened
- 100 g (4 oz) self-raising flour
- 2 tablespoons cocoa powder
- 50 g (2 oz) ground almonds
- 100 g (4 oz) frozen raspberries

For the topping:
- 150 g (5 oz) butter, softened
- 250 g (9 oz) icing sugar
- a few drops of vanilla essence
- 3 drops pink food colouring
- 2 tablespoons hot water
- chocolate stars, to decorate

1 Preheat the oven to 180°C / 350°F / gas mark 4.

2 Place the dark chocolate and water into a small saucepan. Stir over a low heat until melted and smooth. Set aside to cool.

3 Place the eggs, brown sugar and butter in a large mixing bowl. Beat until just combined.

4 Sift in the self-raising flour and cocoa, and add in the ground almonds. Stir well to combine.

5 Add the warm chocolate to the mixture and stir until just combined.

6 Use a teaspoon to transfer equal amounts of the mixture to the bun cases, half filling each case. Place a couple of raspberries in the middle, and then top with the remaining mixture. Bake the cupcakes for about 20–25 minutes. Leave to cool on a wire rack.

7 For the topping, beat together the butter and icing sugar. Once well mixed, add the vanilla essence, food colouring and water. Beat until smooth.

8 Place the topping in a piping bag and swirl over your cupcakes. Decorate with chocolate stars to finish.

CHOCOLATE MACARONS

Extra equipment:
- blender
- piping bag
- baking tray
- baking parchment

Ingredients:
- 140 g (5 oz) ground almonds
- 275 g (9 1/2 oz) icing sugar
- 25 g (1 oz) cocoa powder
- 4 egg whites

For the filling:
- chocolate spread

1 Preheat the oven to 180°C / 350°F / gas mark 4.

2 First, blend the almonds, icing sugar and cocoa powder until very fine. Ask an adult for help with the blender.

3 Next, in a clean bowl, whisk the egg whites until stiff peaks form and then fold into the almond mixture.

4 Then, place into a piping bag and pipe circles onto a baking tray lined with baking parchment. Leave to set for 15 minutes.

5 Place in the oven to bake for 7–8 minutes. Then, remove the macarons from the parchment to cool (see top tip).

6 Once cool, spread the chocolate spread filling onto one macaron, then sandwich with another macaron.

7 Repeat with all of the macarons until they are all used up.

TOP TIP!
To remove the macarons without them sticking or tearing, lift one corner of the parchment and ask an adult to pour boiled water onto the tray. As the water hits the base of the parchment the macarons will lift off easily.

CHOCOLATE TRIFLE

SERVES 4

Extra equipment:
- 4 glass ramekins
- whisk
- grater

Ingredients:
- 170 g (6 oz) white chocolate
- 2 egg yolks
- 25 g (1 oz) caster sugar
- 150 ml (5 fl.oz) milk
- 85 ml (3 fl.oz) double cream
- 4 slices swiss roll
- cocoa powder, to decorate
- dark chocolate, grated, to decorate

1 Break 150 g (5 oz) white chocolate into small pieces, grating the remainder for later.

2 Next, cream the egg yolks and caster sugar together in a large bowl. Whisk for about 2–3 minutes until the mixture is pale, thick and creamy.

3 Pour the milk and double cream into a saucepan and ask an adult to bring to the boil. Pour onto the egg yolk mixture, whisking all the time. Pour back into the pan over a moderate heat. Stir the mixture until it starts to thicken.

4 Add the white chocolate pieces and stir until melted. Then, remove the pan from the heat and allow to cool slightly.

5 Start to place the swiss roll pieces in each of the glass ramekins, then pour the white chocolate mixture over, filling the ramekins to the top. Leave to set in the fridge, preferably overnight.

6 When ready to serve, sprinkle cocoa powder over the top of each ramekin and finish with grated dark chocolate and the white chocolate reserved from earlier.

TOP TIP!
Always ask an adult for help with a grater.

CHOCOLATE MERINGUE NESTS

Extra equipment:
- baking tray
- silicone paper
- piping bag

Ingredients:
- 5 egg whites
- 340 g (12 oz) caster sugar
- 225 g (8 oz) dark chocolate
- 300 ml (10 fl.oz) whipping cream
- ground cinnamon, to taste
- 4 walnut halves

1 Preheat the oven to 110°C / 225°F / gas mark 1/4.

2 Beat the egg whites until they form soft peaks. Gradually beat in the sugar until you have a stiff and shiny meringue mixture.

3 Line a baking tray with silicone paper. Use a piping bag with a medium star nozzle to pipe the meringue out into nests approximately 9 cm (3 1/2 in) in a spiral, starting in the centre. The mixture should produce four nests. Bake in a preheated oven for approximately 2 1/2 hours or until crisp.

4 Ask an adult to melt the dark chocolate over a bowl of warm water and spoon a little into the base of each nest. Allow to set.

5 Beat the whipping cream until half whipped, feed in most of the remaining chocolate and sprinkle with cinnamon.

6 To serve, spoon the mixture into the meringue cases, decorate with the walnut halves and dribble the remaining chocolate over the sides. Dust with cinnamon, to taste.

TOP TIP!
If you have any leftover meringue, crumble it in a bowl and top with fresh berries and cream!

CHOCOLATE ALMOND BARS

Extra equipment:
- 24 cm (9 in) square baking tin
- spatula

Ingredients:
- 125 g (4 $^{1}/_{2}$ oz) soft butter
- 300 g (10 oz) good-quality dark chocolate, broken into pieces
- 3 tablespoons golden syrup
- 150 g (5 oz) almonds

1 First, ask an adult to heat the butter, dark chocolate and golden syrup in a saucepan over a gentle heat. Remove from the heat, scoop out about 125 ml (4$^{1}/_{2}$ fl.oz) of the melted mixture and set aside in a bowl.

2 Next, fold the almonds into the saucepan, then tip the mixture into the square baking tin and smooth the top with a wet spatula.

3 Pour over the reserved melted chocolate mixture and again, smooth the top with a wet spatula.

4 Refrigerate for about two hours or overnight, then serve once set.

TOP TIP!
Why not add marshmallows or biscuits at the same time as the almonds to make rocky road bars?

CHOCOLATE-CHIP COOKIES

Extra equipment:
• baking tray
• sieve

Ingredients:
• 125 g (4 ½ oz) butter
• 100 g (4 oz) caster sugar
• 75 g (3 oz) brown sugar
• 1 egg
• a few drops of vanilla extract
• 150 g (5 oz) plain flour
• ½ teaspoon baking powder
• 50 g (2 oz) chocolate chips

1 Preheat the oven to 180°C / 350°F / gas mark 4.

2 Use a paper towel to grease the baking tray with a little butter.

3 Put the butter and both sugars into a large bowl and mix them together with a wooden spoon until they are light and fluffy.

4 Add the egg and the vanilla extract and beat well.

5 Sift the plain flour and baking powder into the bowl. Stir them into the mixture, then add the chocolate chips.

6 Put 8–10 teaspoons of the mixture onto the greased tray (you will probably have enough mixture for two batches). Bake the cookies for 15–20 minutes or until golden brown.

7 Leave them to cool for 2–3 minutes before lifting them onto a wire rack to cool completely.

TOP TIP! Don't be afraid to experiment with the recipe – add nuts, sweets or more chocolate!

47

XOCOLATL

SERVES 2

Extra equipment:
- sieve
- whisk

Ingredients:
- 500 ml (17 fl.oz) full cream milk
- 1 vanilla pod, split in half
- 1 cinnamon stick
- small pinch of chilli powder
- 150 g (5 oz) dark chocolate, grated or chopped
- honey
- grated chocolate to serve

1 Ask an adult to gently heat the milk with the vanilla, cinnamon stick and chilli powder for one minute.

2 Add the dark chocolate and mix until completely melted.

3 Off the heat, allow the ingredients to infuse for 5–10 minutes.

4 Strain the mixture to remove the vanilla and cinnamon, then gently reheat it, being careful not to let it boil.

5 Add honey to taste.

6 Whisk and serve.

TOP TIP!
Pour into your favourite mug and top with grated chocolate or cocoa powder.

48

CHOCOLATE-CHIP CHEESECAKE

Extra equipment:
- 23 cm (9 in) springform cake tin
- clean plastic bag
- rolling pin

Ingredients:
- 125 g (4 ½ oz) digestive biscuits
- 5 tablespoons caster sugar
- 75 g (3 oz) butter, melted
- 5 tablespoons unsweetened cocoa powder

For the filling:
- 675 g (1 lb 5 oz) cream cheese
- 397 g (14 oz) tin condensed milk
- 2 teaspoons vanilla extract
- 3 eggs
- 120 g (4 ½ oz) chocolate chips
- 1 teaspoon plain flour

To decorate:
- chocolate wafer stick
- runny honey

1 Preheat the oven to 150°C / 300°F / gas mark 2.

2 Place the biscuits in a strong plastic bag and crush them into fine crumbs with a rolling pin.

3 Then, mix the crumbs, sugar, butter and cocoa powder together in a bowl. Press onto the bottom and up the sides of the springform cake tin.

4 To make the filling, put the cream cheese into a bowl, then gradually add the condensed milk, beating well.

5 Next, add the vanilla extract and the eggs, and beat again until smooth.

6 Add the chocolate chips, along with the flour (this keeps them from sinking to the bottom of the cheesecake) and mix well. Pour over the prepared biscuit base.

7 Ask an adult to place in the oven and bake for 1 hour. After an hour, turn off the oven (do not open the oven door) and leave the cake to cool for another hour. Then remove from the oven and cool completely.

8 Refrigerate before removing the sides of the tin. When you're ready to serve, drizzle honey over the top of the cheesecake and top with a chocolate wafer stick.

TOP TIP!
Don't forget to chill the cheesecake afterwards as it needs time to set!

CHOCOLATE & PEANUT BUTTER CUPCAKES

Extra equipment:
- bun tin and bun cases
- piping bag

Ingredients:
- 225 g (8 oz) light brown sugar
- 50 g (2 oz) butter, softened
- 125 g (4 1/2 oz) chocolate spread
- 2 eggs
- a few drops of vanilla extract
- 150 g (5 oz) plain flour
- 75 g (3 oz) cocoa powder
- 2 teaspoons baking powder
- 100 ml (3 fl.oz) milk

For the topping:
- 4 tablespoons butter, softened
- 225 g (8 oz) cream cheese
- 170 g (6 oz) smooth peanut butter
- 350 g (12 oz) icing sugar
- 100 g (4 oz) whipped cream

1 Preheat the oven to 180°C / 350°F / gas mark 4.

2 Beat the light brown sugar and butter together until smooth and then add the chocolate spread and mix together thoroughly.

3 Add the eggs, one at a time, beating well after each addition, and then add the vanilla extract.

4 Sift the flour, cocoa powder and baking powder together and fold into the mixture, along with the milk.

5 Put spoonfuls of the mixture into the bun cases.

6 Bake the cupcakes for 20–25 minutes, then leave them to cool on a wire rack.

7 For the topping, beat the butter, cream cheese, and smooth peanut butter until blended.

8 Add the icing sugar slowly, then add the whipped cream and beat until smooth and creamy.

9 Place the topping into a piping bag and swirl onto each of the cupcakes.

TOP TIP! Sprinkle peanuts on top for a double nut hit!

CHOCOLATE MOUSSE

Extra equipment:
• 4 serving glasses

Ingredients:
• 200 g (7 oz) good-quality dark chocolate, broken into pieces
• 30 ml (1 fl.oz) milk
• 1 teaspoon dark-roast coffee granules
• 5 very fresh free-range eggs, separated
• 50 g (2 oz) grated dark chocolate, to decorate

1 Ask an adult to put the dark chocolate and the milk in a heatproof bowl over a saucepan of barely simmering water. Stir them occasionally.

2 As soon as the chocolate pieces have melted, stir in the coffee granules and ask an adult to immediately remove the pan from the heat.

3 Allow the mixture to cool completely, then stir in the beaten egg yolks.

4 In a clean bowl, beat the egg whites until they form stiff peaks.

5 Gradually and carefully fold the beaten egg whites into the chocolate mixture, a spoonful at a time. Continue until all the egg whites have been used.

6 Spoon the mousse into attractive glasses and refrigerate for three hours. Before serving, sprinkle each mousse with grated dark chocolate.

TOP TIP!
Fresh strawberries make a refreshing addition to this dessert.

CHOCOLATE & ALMOND FRIDGE CAKE

Extra equipment:
- clean plastic bag
- rolling pin
- square tin
- baking parchment

Ingredients:
- 200 g (7 oz) digestive biscuits
- 150 g (5 oz) dark chocolate
- 100 g (4 oz) milk chocolate
- 50 g (2 oz) butter
- 50 g (2 oz) honey
- pinch of cinnamon
- 25 g (1 oz) blanched almonds, roughly chopped
- 50 g (2 oz) candied citrus peel, finely chopped
- icing sugar, to decorate

1 Place the biscuits in a strong plastic bag and crush them roughly with a rolling pin.

2 Break both types of chocolate into small pieces and ask an adult to melt it in a heatproof bowl over a saucepan of simmering water, stirring occasionally. (Make sure that the bowl is not touching the water.)

3 As soon as the chocolate has melted, add the butter, honey and cinnamon. Stir over the heat until well mixed.

4 Take the saucepan off the heat, and add the crushed biscuits, almonds and chopped citrus peel and mix thoroughly.

5 Press into a greased and lined square tin and allow to cool. Chill in the fridge overnight.

6 While still in the tin, cut the fridge cake into thick fingers. (They are best stored in a container in the fridge.)

7 Remove the cake from the fridge fifteen minutes before serving and sprinkle each slice with a little icing sugar.

TOP TIP!
These fridge cake bars freeze well! Just take them out of the freezer a few hours before serving to defrost.

CHOC POPS

Extra equipment:
• jug
• ice lolly moulds

Ingredients:
• 60 g (2 oz) milk chocolate
• 3 tablespoons natural yogurt
• 6 drops vanilla extract
• 2 tablespoons milk

1 Ask an adult to put a heatproof bowl over a saucepan of just-simmering water, making sure the bowl doesn't touch the water. Break the milk chocolate into small pieces and put them into the bowl. Stir the mixture until the chocolate has melted.

2 Pour the melted chocolate into a jug and add the remaining ingredients. Stir, then leave to cool. Once cool, pour the mixture into the ice lolly moulds.

3 Put the moulds into a freezer and allow to set for at least 4 hours, until solid.

4 Remove the lollies from the freezer and let them stand at room temperature for 5 minutes. Then, remove from the moulds and enjoy!

TOP TIP! Add 2 chopped bananas to the mixture for Banana and Chocolate Pops!

CHOCOLATE PARTY BISCUITS

Extra equipment:
- sieve
- cookie cutter
- non-stick baking tray
- piping bag (optional)

Ingredients:
- 250 g (8 ½ oz) butter, softened
- 140 g (4 ½ oz) caster sugar
- 1 egg yolk
- 2 teaspoons vanilla extract
- 300 g (10 ½ oz) plain flour

For the chocolate topping:
- 100 g (4 oz) dark chocolate
- sugar sprinkles (optional)

1 Preheat the oven to 180°C / 350°F / gas mark 4.

2 Mix the butter and sugar in a large bowl with a wooden spoon, then add the egg yolk and vanilla extract and beat to combine.

3 Sift over the plain flour and stir until the mixture is well combined. Don't be afraid to use your hands to give everything a really good mix and press the dough together.

4 Then, roll out the dough and cut out different shapes, either with a cookie cutter or ask an adult to use a sharp knife.

5 Place the shapes on a non-stick baking tray, spaced out and ask an adult to place into the preheated oven for about 12 minutes.

6 Meanwhile, ask an adult to melt the dark chocolate in a bowl over a pan of just-simmering water.

7 Once melted, dip the biscuits into the chocolate or use a piping bag to pipe features, twirls and shapes onto the biscuits and then top with sugar sprinkles. Leave to set, then serve!

TOP TIP! Substitute 50 g (2 oz) cocoa powder for 50 g (2 oz) of the plain flour to make double chocolate biscuits!

CHOCOLATE CELEBRATION CAKE

Extra equipment:
- 23 cm (9 in) springform cake tin
- sieve
- grater

Ingredients:
- 250 g (9 oz) butter
- 400 g (14 oz) caster sugar
- 5 free-range eggs, beaten
- 150 ml (5 fl.oz) sour cream
- 300 g (10 oz) plain flour
- 100 g (4 oz) cocoa powder
- 50 g (2 oz) ground almonds
- 1 teaspoon baking powder
- ¹/₂ teaspoon bicarbonate of soda

For the filling:
- 100 g (4 oz) unsalted butter
- 200 g (7 oz) icing sugar
- 4 tablespoons cocoa powder
- drop of milk
- 75 g (3 oz) grated dark chocolate, to decorate

1 Preheat the oven to 160°C / 325°F / gas mark 3. Grease a 23 cm (9 in) springform cake tin with a little butter.

2 Cream the butter and sugar together until the mixture is pale and fluffy. Add the beaten eggs a little at a time, mixing well, then add the sour cream.

3 Sift the plain flour, cocoa powder, ground almonds, baking powder and bicarbonate of soda, holding the sieve up high to allow as much air into the ingredients as possible. Fold them into the cake mixture gently.

4 Transfer the mixture to the cake tin and bake for about 90 minutes. Allow the cake to cool in the tin for ten minutes, then transfer it to a cooling rack.

5 Once cool, ask an adult to cut it into three or four layers.

6 To make the filling, place the butter in a bowl, then gradually sift and beat in the icing sugar and cocoa powder, then enough milk to make the mixture fluffy. Refrigerate for 30 minutes before using.

7 Spread the filling onto the bottom layer of the cake and place the next layer on top. Continue, spreading the filling between each layer.

8 Decorate the top and sides of the cake with the remaining filling and top with curls or shavings of dark chocolate (ask an adult to help you use a grater).

TOP TIP!
Single cream is the perfect accompaniment for this dessert.

CHOCOLATE APPLES

Extra equipment:
- 12 wooden sticks
- greaseproof paper

Ingredients:
- 12 dessert apples, peeled
- 1 kg (2 lb 2 oz) milk chocolate, chopped

For the topping:
- sugar sprinkles
- chopped nuts
- melted chocolate

1 Ask an adult to insert the wooden sticks into the cores of the apples at the stem.

2 Next, ask an adult to put a heatproof bowl over a saucepan of just-simmering water. Make sure the bowl doesn't touch the water. Break the chocolate into small pieces and put them in the bowl. Stir until the chocolate has melted, then remove from the heat.

3 Next, dip the peeled apples into the melted chocolate, turning to coat completely.

4 Then, dip or roll the apples in your selected topping, and place on a sheet of greaseproof paper. Repeat with the remaining apples.

5 Allow the chocolate covering to set at room temperature. Check to make sure it is firm before serving.

TOP TIP!
Experiment with the toppings and also the chocolate. Why not try white or dark?

56

MARBLE CAKE

Extra equipment:
- 1 kg (2 lb) loaf tin
- baking parchment
- skewer

Ingredients:
- 150 g (5 oz) butter, softened
- 150 g (5 oz) caster sugar
- 3 eggs
- 150 g (5 oz) self-raising flour
- 3 tablespoons milk
- 1 teaspoon vanilla extract
- 2 tablespoons cocoa powder

1 Preheat the oven to 180°C / 350°F / gas mark 4.

2 Grease the inside of a loaf tin with a little butter. Then, place it over a sheet of baking parchment and draw around it. Ask an adult to cut the rectangle out, then place it inside the loaf tin to line the base. Then, cut strips of baking parchment to line the sides of the tin.

3 Put the butter and sugar in a bowl and beat together. Next, add the eggs, one at a time, mixing well. Carefully fold in the flour, milk and vanilla extract until smooth.

4 Divide the mixture between two bowls. Stir the cocoa powder into one of the bowls.

5 Next, take two spoons and alternately place the vanilla mixture and the chocolate mixture into the loaf tin. Once all of the mixtures have been used up, bang the tin on a work surface to get rid of any air bubbles.

6 Use a skewer to swirl the mixtures around in the loaf tin to create a marbled effect.

7 Bake in the preheated oven for 1–1¼ hours, until the cake feels firm to the touch. Then, turn out onto a wire rack to cool.

TOP TIP!
Ask an adult to insert a skewer into the cake when cooked – if it comes out clean, it's ready!

MINT CHOCOLATE CUPCAKES

TOP TIP!
Experiment with bun cases. Keep an eye out for unusual cases in kitchen accessory and homeware shops.

Extra equipment:
- bun tin and bun cases
- sieve

Ingredients:
- 60 g (2 oz) dark chocolate
- 150 ml (5 fl.oz) water
- 2 eggs
- 150 g (5 oz) brown sugar
- 1/4 teaspoon peppermint essence
- 90 g (4 oz) butter, softened
- 125 g (4 oz) self-raising flour
- 2 tablespoons cocoa powder
- 30 g (1 oz) ground almonds

For the topping:
- 150 g (5 oz) butter, softened
- 250 g (9 oz) icing sugar
- a few drops of vanilla essence
- 2 drops green food colouring
- chocolate curls, to decorate

1 Preheat the oven to 175°C / 350°F / gas mark 4. Put the paper cases in the bun tin.

2 Place the dark chocolate and water into a small saucepan. Ask an adult to stir over a low heat until melted and smooth. Set aside to cool.

3 Place the eggs, brown sugar, peppermint essence and butter in a large mixing bowl. Beat until light and fluffy.

4 Sift in the self-raising flour and cocoa powder. Add the ground almonds. Stir well to combine.

5 Add the warm chocolate to the mixture and stir until just combined.

6 Use a teaspoon to transfer equal amounts of the mixture to the paper cases. Bake the cupcakes for about 25–30 minutes. Leave them to cool on a wire rack.

7 For the topping, beat together the butter and icing sugar. Once well mixed, add the vanilla essence and food colouring. Add 2 teaspoons of hot water and beat until smooth and creamy.

8 Swirl over your cupcakes. Decorate with chocolate curls.

HOT CHOCA MOCHA

Ingredients:

- 100 g (4 oz) dark chocolate, grated or chopped
- 50 g (2 oz) sugar
- large cup of strong black espresso
- hot water to taste
- single cream, to decorate

1 Ask an adult to gently heat the dark chocolate, sugar and espresso with some water to taste.

2 Mix until completely dissolved.

3 Serve in warmed cups and top with the single cream.

TOP TIP! Serve with another fabulous chocolate recipe from this book!

CHOCOLATE EGGS

TOP TIP!
Collect some brightly coloured foil and wrap your home-made eggs – they make great presents!

MAKES 8

Extra equipment:
- 8 small chocolate egg moulds
- cooking thermometer
- greaseproof paper
- palette knife
- foil (optional)

Ingredients:
- 300 g (10 oz) good-quality plain chocolate
- sunflower oil, for polishing moulds

1 Dampen a piece of kitchen towel with a little sunflower oil, and polish the inside of each mould.

2 Next, break the chocolate into small, even pieces and ask an adult to melt gently in a bowl over a saucepan of hot water, making sure the bowl is not touching the water. Place a cooking thermometer into the chocolate and heat until it reaches 43°C / 110°F. Then, take off the heat and cool to 35°C / 95°F.

3 Pour spoonfuls of the chocolate into each mould and swirl around until they are completely coated. Leave to set, flat side down and covered in greaseproof paper. Fill each mould the same way. Leave to set for at least 20 minutes.

4 Repeat the process another two or three times to build up a good layer of chocolate. Ask an adult to draw a palette knife across the edge of the mould to ensure a clean edge. This is important so that the two sides of the egg stick together evenly. Leave to chill until set.

5 Carefully unmould the egg halves, taking care not to handle the chocolate too much as it will start to melt. To stick the two edges of an egg together, heat a baking tray and then place the edges of two halves on it for a few seconds, then gently push the edges together. Take care as the tray will be very hot.

CHOCOLATE PINWHEEL COOKIES

Extra equipment:
- cling film
- rolling pin

Ingredients:
- 200 g (7 oz) unsalted butter
- 150 g (5 oz) caster sugar
- 2 teaspoons vanilla extract
- 1 egg
- 300 g (10 oz) plain flour, sifted
- 25 g (1 oz) cocoa powder

1 Preheat the oven to 180°C / 350°F / gas mark 4.

2 Put the butter and sugar in the bowl and mix together well. Next, beat in the vanilla and egg, then add the flour. Knead until a dough forms, then remove from the bowl.

3 Halve the dough and beat the cocoa powder into one of the portions.

4 Shape both dough portions into rough oblong shapes, then wrap in cling film and put in the fridge for 30 minutes to chill until firm.

5 Once firm, roll out each dough portion, trying to maintain the oblong shape.

6 Put the chocolate dough on top of the vanilla dough and ask an adult to trim the edges to neaten. Roll up lengthways, then wrap in cling film and chill again for 45 minutes.

7 Ask an adult to slice the dough into discs, then put them on a baking tray, spacing them out evenly. Cook for 15 minutes, then turn out to cool on a wire rack.

TOP TIP!
Serve these delicious cookies with vanilla ice cream!

CHOCOLATE RICE PUDDING

Extra equipment:

- whisk
- 8 ramekins

Ingredients:

- 800 ml (27 fl.oz) milk
- 100 g (4 oz) pudding or risotto rice
- 75 g (3 oz) caster sugar
- 25 g (1 oz) cocoa powder
- 1 teaspoon vanilla extract

1 Pour half of the milk into a pan along with the rice and ask an adult to bring to the boil. Turn off the heat, cover with a lid and leave for an hour to let the rice swell and slowly absorb the milk.

2 After the hour has passed, lift off the lid, add the remaining milk, sugar, cocoa powder and vanilla extract, whisk and ask an adult to bring slowly to the boil, stirring often to check that it's not sticking to the pan.

3 Keep the pan at a gentle boil for about 15 minutes, stirring every few minutes. Then, remove from the heat, pop the lid back on and leave for another 30–60 minutes.

4 If you would like the pudding to be of a thinner consistency, add additional milk or single cream.

5 Pour into the individual ramekins, and place in a fridge to cool before serving.

TOP TIP!
Top the rice puddings with flaked almonds, mint leaves and a couple of raspberries!

CHOCOLATE PROFITEROLES

Extra equipment:
- greaseproof paper
- piping bag
- whisk

Ingredients:
- 125 ml (4 fl.oz) milk
- 200 ml (6 ½ fl.oz) water
- 1 teaspoon golden caster sugar
- 100 g (4 oz) butter
- 150 g (5 oz) plain flour, sifted
- 4 eggs, lightly beaten

For the cream:
- 300 ml (10 fl.oz) whipping cream
- 15 g (½ oz) caster sugar
- a few drops of vanilla essence

For the chocolate sauce:
- 200 g (7 oz) dark chocolate
- 25 g (1 oz) unsalted butter
- 3 tablespoons clear honey
- 125 ml (4 fl.oz) full fat milk

1 Preheat the oven to 180°C / 350°F / gas mark 4.

2 Place the milk, cold water and sugar into a pan and ask an adult to heat. Once the sugar has dissolved, add the butter and stir until melted. Bring to a boil, then turn off the heat and tip in the flour. Beat with a wooden spoon for a couple of minutes, before pouring onto a plate to cool. Once cool, return the mixture to the pan, then gradually beat in the eggs, a little at a time, mixing well until you have a smooth choux pastry paste.

3 Line a baking tray with greaseproof paper. Spoon the choux pastry into a piping bag and pipe about 20 small balls onto the baking tray, spaced well apart.

4 Bake for 18–20 minutes until well risen and golden brown. Remove from the oven and transfer to a wire rack to cool.

5 Whip the cream, caster sugar and vanilla essence until stiff enough to pipe and, using a clean piping bag with a small plain nozzle, cut each profiterole in half and fill the middle with cream.

6 For the sauce, ask an adult to put a heatproof bowl over a saucepan of just-simmering water. Make sure the bowl doesn't touch the water. Break the chocolate into small pieces and put them in the bowl. Add the butter and honey, stirring until the chocolate has melted, then whisk in the milk until you have a smooth sauce.

TOP TIP! Serve the profiteroles with the hot chocolate sauce drizzled all over.

INDEX OF RECIPES

Baci di Dama	36	Choc Pops	53
Berry & White Chocolate Muffins	16	Chocolate Pots	40
Chocolate Almond Bars	46	Chocolate Profiteroles	63
Chocolate & Almond Fridge Cake	52	Chocolate & Raspberry Cake	38
Chocolate Apples	56	Chocolate Rice Pudding	62
Chocolate Celebration Cake	55	Chocolate Roulade	14
Chocolate-Chip Cheesecake	49	Chocolate Soufflé	22
Chocolate-Chip Cookies	47	Chocolate Trifle	44
Chocolate-Chip Cupcakes	27	Chocolate Tartlets	28
Chocolate Coated Nuts	34	Chocolate Truffles	13
Chocolate Eggs	60	Classic Hot Chocolate	37
Chocolate Florentines	24	Courgette & Chocolate Loaf	20
Chocolate Fondue	18	Fruity Chocolate Crumble	33
Chocolate Fudge Brownies	41	Hot Choca Mocha	59
Chocolate & Ginger Cheesecake	11	Hot Chocolate Ice Cream Cake	32
Chocolate Ice Cream	26	Marble Cake	57
Chocolate Ice Cream Sundae	39	Mini Chocolate Cupcakes	35
Chocolate Macarons	43	Mini Chocolate Meringues	15
Chocolate Meringue Nests	45	Mint Chocolate Cupcakes	58
Chocolate Milkshake	19	Nutty Chocolate Fudge	25
Chocolate Mousse	51	Raspberry Chocolate Cupcakes	42
Chocolate & Orange Cookies	10	Sicilian Cassata	21
Chocolate Pancakes	31	Viennese Hot Chocolate	12
Chocolate Party Biscuits	54	White Chocolate Cake	23
Chocolate & Peanut Butter Cookies	30	White Chocolate & Exotic Fruit Cookies	17
Chocolate & Peanut Butter Cupcakes	50	White Chocolate Pistachio Mousse	29
Chocolate Pinwheel Cookies	61	Xocolatl	48

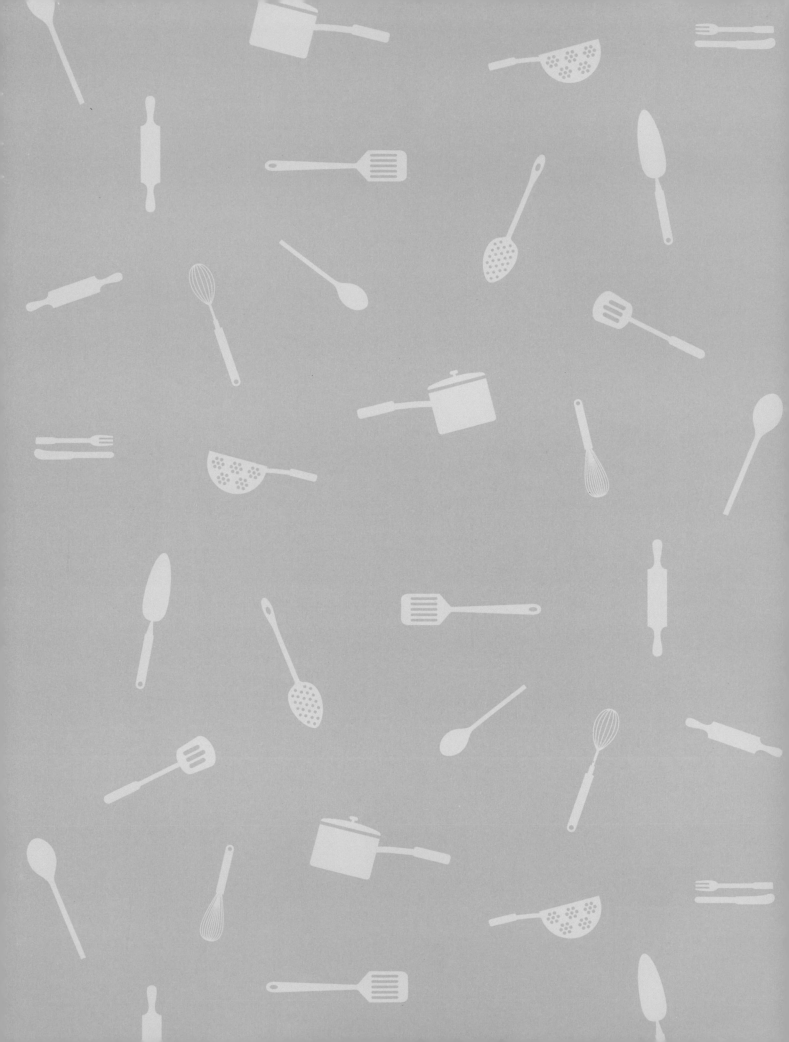